WE THE PEOPLE

The Mayflower Compact

by Philip Brooks

Content Adviser: Julie Richter, Ph.D.,
Independent Scholar and Consultant,
Colonial Williamsburg Foundation

Reading Adviser: Rosemary G. Palmer, Ph.D.,
Department of Literacy, College of Education,
Boise State University

COMPASS POINT BOOKS
MINNEAPOLIS, MINNESOTA

Compass Point Books
3109 West 50th Street, #115
Minneapolis, MN 55410

Visit Compass Point Books on the Internet at *www.compasspointbooks.com*
or e-mail your request to *custserv@compasspointbooks.com*

On the cover: Passengers sign the Mayflower Compact.

Photographs ©: Library of Congress, cover, 17, 29, 33; Bettmann/Corbis, 4, 9, 11, 15, 31; Stock Montage, Inc., 5, 35, 38; Sandro Vannini/Corbis, 6; Photograph courtesy of Andrew Nicholson, 7; Mary Evans Picture Library, 8; North Wind Picture Archives, 10, 13, 30, 32, 36, 37, 39; Hulton/Archive by Getty Images, 12, 20, 22; Photodisc, 18, 19; Joseph Sohm; ChromoSohm Inc./Corbis, 21; Museum of the City of New York/Corbis, 23; Burstein Collection/Corbis, 24, 28; The Granger Collection, New York, 25, 27; Jana Birchum/Getty Images, 40; Kevin Fleming/Corbis, 41.

Creative Director: Terri Foley
Managing Editor: Catherine Neitge
Photo Researcher: Marcie C. Spence
Designer/Page production: Bradfordesign, Inc./Jaime Martens
Cartographer: XNR Productions, Inc.

Library of Congress Cataloging-in-Publication Data
Brooks, Philip, 1963-
   The Mayflower Compact / by Philip Brooks.
      p. cm. — (We the people)
   Includes bibliographical references (p.) and index.
   ISBN 0-7565-0681-6 (hardcover)
1. Mayflower Compact (1620)—Juvenile literature. 2. Mayflower (Ship)—Juvenile literature.
3. Pilgrims (New Plymouth Colony)—Juvenile literature. 4. Massachusetts—History—New Plymouth, 1620-1691—Juvenile literature. [1. Mayflower Compact (1620) 2. Mayflower (Ship)
3. Pilgrims (New Plymouth Colony) 4. Massachusetts—History—New Plymouth, 1620-1691.]
I. Title. II. We the people (Series) (Compass Point Books)
   F68.B867 2004
   974.4'02—dc22   2003024188

TABLE OF CONTENTS

The First Step 4

Voyage of the *Mayflower* 10

The Mayflower Compact 16

Plymouth Is Established 23

The First Thanksgiving 28

Governor William Bradford 34

The Legacy of the Mayflower Compact ... 39

Glossary 42

Did You Know? 43

Important Dates 44

Important People 45

Want to Know More? 46

Index 48

NOTE: *In this book, words that are defined in the glossary are in* **bold** *the first time they appear in the text.*

THE FIRST STEP

A simple document signed in 1620 was the first written outline for government in the New World. William Bradford's Mayflower Compact established the tradition of elected representatives serving in government. This historical agreement was the first step in a long process that eventually led to the writing of the U.S. Constitution nearly 200 years later. At the time, however, it was only

William Bradford signs the Mayflower Compact.

meant to keep peace among colonists in what would become the United States.

The story of the Mayflower Compact begins in England. For centuries, the Roman Catholic Church was the official Church of England. The church helped run the country, and English leaders looked to the pope in Rome, Italy, for religious guidance. In 1534,

King Henry VIII

King Henry VIII changed that. He wanted to divorce his wife and remarry, hoping a new wife would give birth to a son. The pope refused to grant the divorce. For that reason and others, Henry VIII abandoned the Roman Catholic Church. He put himself in charge of the Church of England and made many changes. He closed Catholic monasteries and took away church lands.

Henry VIII enlarged the Chapel Royal at Hampton Court Palace in London.

Because Henry VIII enjoyed the elaborate rituals of the Roman Catholic Church, he did little to change them. Some people felt this new church should be made simpler and more humble. They believed the Church of England needed to be "purified." These **dissenters** became known as **Puritans,** and they hoped to reform the church from within. When church leaders refused to simplify church ceremony and tradition, some dissenters decided to form their own church.

The first **separatist** church was created in Scrooby, a small town in the county of Nottinghamshire, England, in the very early 1600s. In Scrooby, the separatists elected their own church officials and created their own religious rules and traditions, with little regard for the laws of the main church. By 1607, traditional church officials began to **persecute** the new church's leaders. They claimed the separatists had broken English law by ignoring their authority and forming their own congregation.

The dissenters separated from St. Wilfred's Church in Scrooby.

7

The separatists left England for Holland.

In 1608, the separatists decided to move to Holland (also known as the Netherlands) where they would be allowed to worship as they pleased. William Brewster, an organizer of the Scrooby church, financed the trip.

Though they were allowed to do as they wished in Holland, many of the separatists missed England. Most were poor, and they were unhappy their children spoke more Dutch than English. Also, a coming war between the Netherlands and Spain threatened to create danger and more economic hardship.

Church leaders, among them William Brewster and William Bradford, decided that the congregation would leave Europe and go to North America. In this new territory, they would be under the protection of England but able to worship as they saw fit. Bradford was the first to call himself and his fellow separatists **Pilgrims.** He would be instrumental in the success of the new colony.

The Pilgrims prayed as they got ready to go to North America.

VOYAGE OF THE *MAYFLOWER*

On a warm August day in 1620, more than 100 men, women, and children boarded two ships bound for the New World. They hoped the *Speedwell* and *Mayflower* would carry them to a better life in what many years later would become the United States of America.

Not all of the passengers sought religious freedom. Many made the trip in search of economic opportunity. Some were farmworkers who wanted land of their own.

Passengers prepared to board the Speedwell.

All left behind the only lives they had ever known. They headed for the vast wilderness of Virginia with only what they could carry aboard the small ships. At the time, Virginia was a huge territory that included much of the eastern coast of the present-day United States.

The Mayflower *at sea*

It was already late in the sailing season. The Atlantic Ocean would soon be stormy. Indeed, no sooner had they set out than the *Speedwell* sprang leaks that were bad enough to send the two ships back to port. Eventually, the *Mayflower* set out alone.

The Virginia Company of London owned all of the land in Virginia. The company granted members of the

11

Mayflower's passenger list the right to establish a settlement there. Investors hoped to make money when settlers would send valuable products like beaver and otter skins back to England to sell. The colony never made much

12

The Virginia Company of London's coat of arms

money for its original investors, but it would ultimately lead to a new and powerful nation being formed.

Peregrine White's parents brought his cradle from Holland.

A few days into the Atlantic crossing, the *Mayflower* sailed into storms that tossed the small ship until one of its main beams bowed and cracked. The ship began to leak and was in danger of breaking up. A carpenter and some passengers managed to repair the broken beam using materials onboard. During their 65 days at sea, two people died and two were born. Oceanus Hopkins was born at sea. Peregrine White was born while the ship was anchored near Cape Cod, in what is now Massachusetts.

The fact that baby Peregrine was born near Cape Cod is significant. Captain Christopher Jones had hoped to anchor the *Mayflower* near the Hudson River, but the ship had been blown off course and had landed far north of where it was supposed to be. The Virginia Company's land grant stated that the settlement was to be built near the Hudson River. Legally, the *Mayflower's* passengers had no right to settle in what is today Massachusetts.

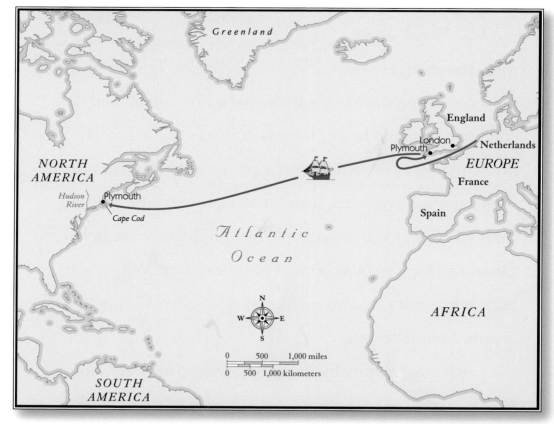

A map of the Mayflower's *voyage*

The Pilgrims landed far north of where they expected.

According to William Bradford's famous account called *History of Plymouth Plantation,* all of the passengers were relieved the trip was over. "Being thus arrived in good harbor and brought safe to land, they fell upon their knees and blessed the God of heaven, who had brought them over the vast and furious ocean," wrote Bradford.

THE MAYFLOWER COMPACT

The *Mayflower* anchored at Cape Cod, well north of its original destination. While scouting the area for a suitable place to build a settlement, many of the Pilgrims onboard grew worried. Their land grant from the Virginia Company did not actually give them any right to the land they planned to settle. The separatists worried that if they established a colony without legal authority, many of the passengers who did not share their religious convictions would leave the group and strike out on their own. This would weaken the new colony.

It was decided an agreement would be written and signed that would create a colonial government with legal authority. When the ship finally docked at Provincetown on November 11, 1620, the Mayflower Compact was signed by 41 of the 102 passengers. Thirty-seven of the signers were separatists. The

Separatists and "strangers" signed the Mayflower Compact.

remaining four men were "strangers," which the separatists
called passengers not in their congregation. Women were
not allowed to sign the document because they had no
legal rights.

The agreement established a temporary government,
which they called a Civil Body Politick, of the Plymouth
Colony. (In December, the Pilgrims would leave
Provincetown and settle in Plymouth, their permanent
colony.) They used their own churches as a model for the new
government. Separatist congregations governed themselves,
directly electing their ministers and church officials.

In the name of God, amen. We, whose names are underwritten, the Loyal Subjects of our dread Sovereign Lord King James, by the Grace of God, of Great Britain, France, and Ireland, King, Defender of the Faith, &c. Having undertaken for the Glory of God, and Advancement of the Christian Faith, and the Honour of our King and Country, a Voyage to plant the first Colony in the northern Parts of Virginia; Do by these Presents, solemnly and mutually, in the Presence of God and one another, covenant and combine ourselves together into a civil Body Politick, for our better Ordering and Preservation, and Furtherance of the Ends aforesaid: And by Virtue hereof do enact, constitute, and frame, such just and equal Laws, Ordinances, Acts, Constitutions, and Officers, from time to time, as shall be thought most meet and convenient for the general Good of the Colony; unto which we promise all due Submission and Obedience.

In witness whereof we have hereunto subscribed our names at Cape-Cod the eleventh of November, in the Reign of our Sovereign Lord King James, of England, France, and Ireland, the eighteenth, and of Scotland the fifty-fourth, Anno Domini; 1620.

John Carver,
William Bradford,
Edward Winslow,
William Brewster,
Isaac Allerton,
Miles Standish,
John Alden,
John Turner,
Francis Eaton,
James Chilton,
John Craxton,
John Billington,
Moses Fletcher,
John Goodman,

Samuel Fuller,
Christopher Martin,
William Mullins,
William White,
Richard Warren,
John Howland,
Stephen Hopkins,
Digery Priest,
Thomas Williams,
Gilbert Winslow,
Edmund Margeson,
Peter Brown,
Richard Britteridge,
George Soule,

Edward Tilly,
John Tilly,
Francis Cooke,
Thomas Rogers,
Thomas Tinker,
John Ridgdale,
Edward Fuller,
Richard Clark,
Richard Gardiner,
John Allerton,
Thomas English,
Edward Doten,
Edward Liester

The words of the Mayflower Compact and the names of the men who signed it

The compact was signed in the cabin of the Mayflower.

Following the signing, John Carver was elected the first governor of the Plymouth Colony. Carver was a wealthy merchant who had helped pay for the *Mayflower's* voyage. He died in April 1621, after serving as governor for less than a year.

The compact became the New World's first written constitution. It established the tradition of elected representative government in the New World. When the colony was first established, all of the colony's men who were not servants (called freemen) attended regular General Court meetings.

The Pilgrim Monument in Provincetown at the tip of Cape Cod marks the site where the Pilgrims signed the Mayflower Compact.

21

They elected the governor and other officials and made laws. Any freeman who failed to attend a General Court meeting received a heavy fine.

By 1638, as the colony expanded and divided, each village elected a representative to attend the General Court meetings in Plymouth. Gradually, the General Court came to have more power than the governor, including the right to tax, make laws, and declare war.

Copies of the signatures on the Mayflower Compact

PLYMOUTH IS ESTABLISHED

On December 26, 1620, the Puritans and their fellow passengers docked near Plymouth, which is 34 miles (54 kilometers) southeast of present-day Boston. Scouts had discovered some cleared land, a stream with fresh water, and a high hill that could be protected from attack. A Native American village once stood at that spot before nearly all its residents were killed by an **epidemic** in 1617.

A Currier & Ives print depicts the landing of the Pilgrims at Plymouth.

23

A large supply of corn, which was a food previously unknown to Europeans, had been left behind and helped the settlers survive the winter.

The *Mayflower's* captain, Christopher Jones, volunteered to stay the winter in Plymouth with his ship. Thanks to Jones, the settlers had shelter during the terribly difficult winter. Still, shortages of food, exhausting work, and brutal cold led to much suffering among the new colonists. Fifty-two died, including Governor John Carver.

The Mayflower *in Plymouth Harbor*

Squanto was a Patuxet Wampanoag.

Thirteen of the 26 fathers and 14 of the 18 mothers aboard the ship died during that first winter. By spring, only a few strong and healthy men and boys were alive to plant crops.

It was at this point that a Patuxet Wampanoag came to Plymouth's rescue. Different sources tell different stories about Squanto, but a few facts are clear. He had been kidnapped and taken to Spain as a slave by an English ship's captain. He learned to speak some English before being returned to his native land. When the Pilgrims arrived and established Plymouth, he taught them to catch fish for use as crop fertilizers. He helped them plant corn, pumpkins, and beans and showed them where to pick berries.

Squanto served as an interpreter and helped bring about a long period of peaceful relations between the local Indian population and the new settlers. Two years after the *Mayflower* landed, Squanto died of smallpox he caught while working as a guide and interpreter for a Pilgrim expedition across Cape Cod.

William Bradford wrote of Squanto's value to the Pilgrims in his history of Plymouth: "Squanto continued with them and was their interpreter and was a special instrument sent of God for their good beyond their expectation. He directed them how to set their corn, where to take fish, and to procure other commodities, and was also their pilot to bring them to unknown places for their profit, and never left them till he died."

Squanto showed the Pilgrims how to use fish as crop fertilizers.

THE FIRST THANKSGIVING

A number of myths have been created around the first Thanksgiving. For instance, the pictures we often see of Pilgrims in black and white clothing with large buckles on their hats and belts are inaccurate. Buckles became fashionable much later. Black and white clothing was commonly worn only on Sundays or during formal

This popular 1914 painting by Jennie Brownscombe was printed in Life *magazine. It is the image many Americans have of the first Thanksgiving.*

The first Thanksgiving was celebrated in 1621.

occasions. Women typically wore red, dark green, brown, blue, violet, and gray dresses. Men wore clothing that was white, beige, black, dark green, and brown.

The most American of holidays actually began as an English tradition. Villages throughout England would come together for feast days of thanksgiving whenever it seemed that God had been particularly merciful. In fall of 1621, the Plymouth colony celebrated their good harvest with a Thanksgiving feast.

Edward Winslow, one of the colony's leaders, wrote of the feast in a letter to England: "Our harvest being gotten in, our Governor sent four men on fowling [bird hunting], that so we might after a more special manner rejoice together. … The four [men] in one day killed as much fowl as … served the company [settlers]

Edward Winslow

almost a week. At which time, amongst other recreations, we exercised our arms [weapons], many of the Indians coming amongst us, and amongst the rest their greatest king Massasoit with some 90 men, whom for three days we entertained and feasted. And they went out and killed five deer which they brought to the plantation [Plymouth] and bestowed on our Governor and upon the Captain and others."

The letter confirms that white settlers and Indians got along well at the time. They ate and celebrated together while carrying their weapons. Massasoit was actually the chief of the Wampanoag tribe that lived in villages throughout much of today's Rhode Island and Massachusetts. The tribe remained at peace with European settlers until Massasoit's death in 1661.

Massasoit maintained peaceful relations with the Pilgrims until he died.

31

Many Wampanoag died from smallpox, which they caught from Europeans.

In the years following that first Thanksgiving gathering, the Wampanoag tribe suffered several terrible epidemics that killed many in the tribe. Europeans carried germs that were unknown in the New World. Such germs were often deadly to Native Americans, who had never been exposed to them.

Metacomet, Massasoit's son and the new chief, decided the tribe had to kill or drive out white settlers or risk disappearing altogether. Their numbers already reduced by the smallpox disease, the Wampanoag and neighboring tribes were no match for English guns. This devastating conflict of 1675 and 1676 was called King Philip's War, after the English name for Metacomet. Most of the Native Americans were killed or took refuge among other tribes. Relations between Native Americans and settlers were never again as friendly as during the Thanksgiving feast of 1621.

Metacomet was also known as Philip.

33

GOVERNOR WILLIAM BRADFORD

The Mayflower Compact did not stop all squabbling and arguing among the settlers. William Bradford wrote: "In these hard and difficult beginnings they found some discontents and murmurings arise amongst some, and mutinous speeches and carriages in other." It was largely John Carver's wise leadership that kept the group together in the first days of Plymouth. "[Arguments and fights] were soon quelled and overcome by the wisdom, patience, and just and equal carriage of things, by the Governor and better part, which clave faithfully together in the main."

After Carver's death, Bradford became governor, and his excellent leadership kept the Pilgrims together. Part of his brilliance as a leader was his flexibility. He was a deeply religious man who saw his task as carrying out God's will. Because of this, one might assume he would believe there was only one way to go about things.

Governor John Carver, shown here meeting with Massasoit, is credited with
keeping the Pilgrims working together in the early days.

35

Governor William Bradford was a wise, practical man.

Instead, Bradford always sought a just and practical solution to each problem the Pilgrims faced.

One difficulty encountered early on was the way in which settlers shared their resources. It was originally decided that all of the Pilgrims would work and farm together for the common good. Everything would be shared equally among all.

36

Bradford saw that although this would work in a perfect world, it led to disputes among the Pilgrims. In his book, he wrote of the problem that "young men, that were most able and fit for labor and service" were unhappy that "they should spend their time and strength to work for other men's wives and children." Women felt the same way about cooking and cleaning for men who were not their husbands.

Pilgrims worked together to build houses in Plymouth.

37

Governor Bradford saw that this is simply how human beings behave. He did not argue with Plymouth's citizens. He did not tell them that God demanded they get along and share everything. Instead, he decided that it was God who had created people with a desire to own their own land and work for themselves. This, it seemed to Bradford, was God's plan. By giving each family their own home and piece of land to farm, Plymouth stood the best chance of survival. Such decisions were the mark of his 30 years as governor.

A statue of William Bradford

38

THE LEGACY OF
THE MAYFLOWER COMPACT

The original Mayflower Compact signed aboard the ship has been lost without a trace, but its principles remain part of the present-day United States. The simple document bound together a group of settlers with various interests and differing religious beliefs. It established that written laws would be just as important in the New World as they had been in the old. The structure of government it provided held strong during Plymouth's worst times. It is a credit to the settlers themselves that despite some arguments and grumbling, the rule of law was always followed.

The first page of William Bradford's history book, which also contained the wording of the Mayflower Compact

Many distinguished Americans can trace their roots directly to members of the *Mayflower's* passenger list. Presidents whose relatives helped found Plymouth include John Adams, John Quincy Adams, Zachary Taylor, Ulysses S. Grant, James Garfield, and Franklin Delano Roosevelt. President George W. Bush and his father, former President George H. W. Bush, and mother, Barbara, all trace their lineage to Plymouth. It is interesting to note that the man whose line eventually led to the two presidents almost died at sea during the voyage. John Howland fell overboard during a storm at sea and was rescued.

As to what happened to the *Mayflower* after its historic journey,

The Bush family traces its lineage to Plymouth.

The Mayflower II *is docked in Plymouth.*

little is known. In 1957, a replica of the ship was built using information about what similar English merchant ships looked like. The *Mayflower II* became a gift from the British to the Americans. Following its creation, it crossed the Atlantic. Sailors found it hard to steer and were nervous when it rolled rather wildly with the sea. In 1995, the ship set sail once again to commemorate the 375th anniversary of the original ship's arrival in the New World. The ship is now docked in Plymouth as part of a museum.

41

GLOSSARY

dissenters—people who refuse to accept the teachings or rules of an official state church or political institution

epidemic—severe outbreak of an infectious disease that is often fatal

persecute—to continually treat in a cruel and unfair way

Pilgrims—dissenting Puritans who came to North America to start their own church, separate from the established Church of England; they founded the Plymouth Colony

Puritans—members of a reform movement who wished to purify the Church of England from within and not separate from it; they founded the Massachusetts Bay Colony

separatist—a person who chooses to separate or break away from an established church or nation

DID YOU KNOW?

- No one knows what happened to the *Mayflower*. The last record of the ship was made in 1624. Then she disappeared from shipping records. Several people in England claim to have pieces of the famous ship but there is no real proof.

- Most Pilgrim families left their daughters in England with plans to send for them later. They believed that girls' bodies would be too weak to survive the first winter in the New World. In fact, girls survived the cold and hunger at higher rates than Pilgrim men, women, or boys.

- Most married women in Plymouth Colony would have a child every two or three years for as long as they were able. Families with eight or 10 children were not uncommon. Sadly, many of the young children died.

- If you can trace your family tree back to a member of the *Mayflower's* passenger list, you can join the Mayflower Society. Today, millions of Americans are direct descendents of the original handful of Pilgrims.

IMPORTANT DATES

Timeline

1620	The *Mayflower* docks near present-day Cape Cod, and the Mayflower Compact is signed.
1621	Squanto arrives at Plymouth Colony to aid the settlers; a peace treaty between the Wampanoag and colonists is signed; Massasoit and 90 men celebrate the first Thanksgiving with the colonists.
1657	Governor William Bradford dies after providing more than 30 years of leadership.
1661	The death of Chief Massasoit ends an era of peaceful relations between his Wampanoag tribe and the Pilgrims.
1675–1676	Native Americans lose King Philip's War to the colonists.

IMPORTANT PEOPLE

WILLIAM BRADFORD (1590–1657)
Pilgrim leader who was the second governor of the Plymouth Colony and served for 30 years

WILLIAM BREWSTER (1567–1644)
Pilgrim leader and signer of the Mayflower Compact

JOHN CARVER (1576–1621)
First governor of the Plymouth Colony, he died in office and served less than a year

MASSASOIT (1580?–1661)
Wampanoag chief who signed a peace treaty with the Pilgrims in 1621 and attended the first Thanksgiving

METACOMET, ALSO KNOWN AS PHILIP (1639?–1676)
Wampanoag chief and Massasoit's son who fought the Plymouth colonists and lost King Philip's War

SQUANTO (1585?–1622)
Patuxet Wampanoag who befriended the Plymouth colonists

WANT TO KNOW MORE?

At the Library

Carter, E. J. *The Mayflower Compact.* Chicago: Heinemann Library, 2003.

Riehecky, Janet. *The Wampanoag: The People of the First Light.* Mankato, Minn.: Bridgestone Books, 2003.

Santella, Andrew. *The Plymouth Colony.* Minneapolis: Compass Point Books, 2001.

Whitcraft, Melissa. *The Mayflower Compact.* New York: Children's Press, 2003.

On the Web

For more information on the *Mayflower Compact,* use FactHound to track down Web sites related to this book.

1. Go to *www.facthound.com*

2. Type in a search word related to this book or this book ID: 0756506816.

3. Click on the *Fetch It* button.

Your trusty FactHound will fetch the best Web sites for you!

On the Road

Plimoth Plantation Museum

137 Warren Ave.

Plymouth, MA 02360

508/746-1622

To visit a re-creation of circa 1627 Plymouth, a Wampanoag home,
and the *Mayflower II*

Pilgrim Hall Museum

75 Court St.

Plymouth, MA 02360

508/746-1620

To view a collection of Pilgrim possessions and Native American artifacts

INDEX

Adams, John, 40
Adams, John Quincy, 40

Bradford, William, 4, *4*, 9, 15, 26, 34, 36, *36,* 37, 38, *38*
Brewster, William, 8, 9
Bush family, 40, *40*

Cape Cod, Massachusetts, 13, 16, 26
Carver, John, 20, 24, 34, *35*
Church of England, 5
Civil Body Politick, 17
clothing, 28–29
Constitution, 4
corn, 24, 26

England, 5, 7, 8, 9, 29
epidemics, 23, 32, *32*

farming, 10, 26, *27,* 36, 38
food, 24, 26
fur trade, 12–13

Garfield, James, 40
General Court, 20, 22
governors, 20, 22, 24, 34, 36–38
Grant, Ulysses S., 40

Henry VIII, king of England, 5–6, *5*

History of Plymouth Plantation (William Bradford), 15, 26–27, *39*
Holland, 8
Hopkins, Oceanus, 13
Howland, John, 40

Jones, Christopher, 13–14, 24

King Philip's War, 33

map, *14*
Massachusetts, 13–14, 31
Massasoit (Wampanoag chief), 30, 31, *31, 35*
Mayflower, 10, 11, *11,* 13, 14, 16, 20, 24, *24,* 26
Mayflower II, 41, *41*
Mayflower Compact, *4, 18–19, 20, 22*
Metacomet (Wampanoag chief), 33, *33*

Native Americans, 23, 25–26, *25, 27,* 30, 31, *31, 32, 32,* 33, *33, 35*
Netherlands, 8

Pilgrims, 9, *9, 15,* 23, 26, *27, 31,* 34, 36, 37, *37,* 39. *See also* separatists.
Plymouth Colony, 17, 20, 22, *23, 23,* 24, 29, 34, *37,* 38

Provincetown, Massachusetts, 16, 17, *21*
Puritans, 6, 23, *28*

Roman Catholic Church, 5, 6
Roosevelt, Franklin Delano, 40

Scrooby, Nottinghamshire, England, 7, *7*
separatists, 7, 8, *8,* 9, 16, 17, *17.* *See also* Pilgrims.
smallpox, 26, *32,* 33
Speedwell (ship), 10, *10,* 11
Squanto (Native American), *25,* 26–27, *27*
strangers, 17, *17*

Taylor, Zachary, 40
Thanksgiving, 28–31, *28, 29*

Virginia Company of London, 11–12, *12,* 14, 16
Virginia territory, 11–13

Wampanoag Indians, 25, *25,* 26–27, *27,* 30, 31, *31, 32, 32,* 33, *33, 35*
White, Peregrine, 13, *13*
Winslow, Edward, 30, *30*
women, 17, 25, 29, 37

About the Author

Philip Brooks lives in Gambier, Ohio, with his wife, Balinda, along with five tortoises and two parakeets. He writes nonfiction books for young readers as well as fiction for adults. He loves to read, cook, and play basketball.

A CHRONOLOGY OF
ST. PAUL'S LIFE

The following dates are approximate and for many can only be suggestions based on scholarly guesswork. The only certain date is the appearance of Paul before the proconsul Gallio in Corinth, reported in Acts 18:12–17. From an inscription at Delphi, we know that his term of office lasted only one year, from 51 to 52 AD. Other dates for Paul are usually calculated backward and forward from this point.

EVENT:	AD
Paul's Birth	6 to 10
Jesus' Death and Resurrection	30
The Stoning of Stephen	32 to 33
Paul's Conversion	33 or 34
Time in Arabia (Gal 1:17; 2 Cor 11:32)	35 to 38
His Time in Tarsus	38 to 43 or 44
Ministry in Antioch	43 to 45
First Missionary Journey	45 to 48
Council of Jerusalem	48
Second Missionary Journey	49 to 52
First Letter to Thessalonians	50
Second Letter to Thessalonians	51

Time in Corinth	51 to 52
Third Missionary Journey	53 to 56
Letter to Galatians	53
Time in Ephesus	53 to 56
Letter to Philippians	55
First Letter to Corinthians	55
Letter to Philemon	56
Letter to Romans	56
Second Letter to Corinthians	56
Return to Jerusalem	56 or 57
Prison in Caesarea	56 to 58
Journey to Rome	59
Roman Imprisonment	60 to 61
Release? Journey to Spain?	63 to 66
Further Imprisonment and Death	63 to 67

The last period of Paul's life is very uncertain. If Paul was released after the two years' stay in Rome, as Acts 28 implies, then he may have had as much as five years of further ministry in both the areas of Asia and Greece that he had traveled so often, and also possibly a visit to Spain. It would have been in this period that he composed the Letters to the Colossians and Ephesians, and the Pastoral Letters to Timothy and Titus. Many scholars believe, however, that these were written in Paul's name by his disciples after his death.